The
PRAYER
of
HANNAH

CHARACTER SERIES

The
PRAYER
of
HANNAH

Eight Dynamics of Effective Christianity

Kenn Gividen

Just
Folks
Publishing Company
Columbus IN 47201

THE PRAYER OF HANNAH
published by Just Folks Publishing Company

© 2002 by Kenn Gividen
ISBN: 0-9717789-7-3
LCCN 2002090228

First printing, June 2002
Second printing, August 2002

Acknowledgments:
Cover design: Alpha Advertising
Editors: Sheri Conover Sharlow and Lisa Dismore
Author's photo: Cameo Color Photography Studio

Scripture quotations are from the King James Bible.

Just Folks is a registered trademark
of Columbus Marketing Group, Inc.
and is registered in the United States Patent office.
The J is a trademark of Just Folks Publishing Company.
Printed in the United States of America

For information, please write:
Just Folks Publishing Company
P.O. Box 2012
Columbus, IN 47202

TABLE OF CONTENTS

To my family:
Donna,
Laura, Paul, David,
Makayla and Meadow Brook

and to the just folks
at Grace Baptist Church
Columbus, Indiana

Preface

*This book is not merely
about prayer.*

*It explores eight
Christian character traits
that empower the believer,
making answered prayer
a normal part
of everyday living.*

*The prayer of Hannah
is an example of what
God can do
when we apply
His principles.*

Chapter 1

Hannah Prayed

Hannah prayed. God responded. And the course of world history was changed.

It was early Monday morning. The lights from my second story office beamed like a lighthouse through the dark streets of our small Indiana city. It was quiet. I stood staring out my window while amber street lamps glowed through the mist. I love this time of day. This is when I can get alone with God.

There was something about the stillness of that morning that invited soul searching. A curious thought came to mind. What if the President of the United States were to call this morning? The very remoteness of such a possibility caused me to smile. And suppose he were to invite me to the White House in Washington, D.C. His purpose for the invitation? Just to talk to me. He would ask what was on my mind and if there were anything I needed.

I envisioned the presidential limousine gliding down Fifth Street and stopping at the front door of my office. From there I would be whisked off to the airport where I would board Air Force One. Once in the nation's capital, I would be ushered to the Oval Office. At first sight the commander in chief would rise from his desk, smile broadly, and, with hand extended, eagerly invite me into his presence.

Far greater is the honor of kneeling before our heavenly Father.

I realize, of course, how absurd that scenario must seem. But imagine this: The Creator of the Universe is calling right now! He sits in the throne room of heaven, beckoning us to come boldly into His presence. He eagerly anticipates our fellowship and petitions.

We would consider it a great honor if the president were to invite us to Washington. Far greater is the honor of kneeling before our loving Heavenly Father in prayer.

With that thought in mind, I walked over to my prayer chair and reached for my Bible.

Thumbing through its pages, I came to I Samuel chapter one. I sat back and began to read. Here I met a heartbroken woman named Hannah. She was about to teach me the secret of powerful praying.

❧ GIVING BACK TO GOD

As I sat in my office that morning, I imagined Hannah kneeling in prayer. Tears of sorrow flowed from her embittered soul as she cried out to God. This was not merely an emotional outburst. Hannah's sincerity was evident. Read her prayer carefully.

And she vowed a vow,
and said, O LORD of hosts,
if thou wilt indeed look on the affliction
of thine handmaid, and remember me,
and not forget thine handmaid,
but wilt give unto thine handmaid a man child,
then I will give him unto the LORD
all the days of his life,
and there shall no razor
come upon his head.[1]

Did you see it?

Hannah asked God specifically for a son, but not for herself. In essence Hannah prayed, "Lord, give me a son so I can give him back to you. Let the world see that you are God, indeed." God answered that simple prayer. What God did for Hannah 3,000 years ago, He desires to do for you today.

My prayer life would be changed forever.

The dull rumble of a street sweeper lumbering toward Fifth Street momentarily caught my attention. This was obviously not the president's limo.

I lifted my eyes from my Bible to listen as the sweeper drew closer to the building, to my car. I hope he doesn't scratch my fender, I thought. Maybe I should move it to the back lot out of harm's way.

In hindsight I find that thought utterly amazing. I was within moments of learning a vital key to effective praying. My prayer life would be changed forever. Yet, my thoughts were still focused on the temporal.

My mind followed my eyes back to the pages of the Scripture.

Hannah was an ordinary woman who affected world history with a single, unselfish prayer. When God answered Hannah's prayer, He provided more than just a son. He gave her a son who would become one of Israel's greatest leaders. He was last of the judges and the first of the prophets. He anointed kings and delivered his nation from idolatry.

☙ TOTAL COMMITMENT

An often overlooked footnote of history is the significance of her son's name. Rather than choose a common name, she selected one taken from two Hebrews terms meaning "listen to" and "God." When combined, the word essentially means "His name is God!" That word is *Samuel.*[2]

By naming him Samuel, Hannah was acknowledging her vow. She would give her son to the Lord—down to the last detail—including his name. When someone would ask his name, he could only reply, "His name is God!" You could not call Samuel by name without evoking the effect of Hannah's prayer.

The sound of the street sweeper was fading in the distance. I hardly noticed. God had my full attention and was teaching me this valuable lesson: Hannah's prayer was powerful because she asked God to give something *to Himself*. Her desire was to be a willing vessel through which God would be glorified. This is the opposite of how we usually pray. Typically, we ask God to give something to us.

Because you gain nothing, God alone benefits and thereby gets all the glory.

The dynamic of Hannah's prayer raised serious questions in my mind. When was the last time I asked God for something specific so I could return it to Him? When was the last time I asked God to bless me—not for my gain or glory —but that others would see His power?

Consider the end results of such praying. What if God's answer is "No, I will not give you that which you ask"? You have gained nothing. You have lost nothing.

14

On the other hand, suppose God answers, "Yes, I will give you your request"?

Again, you have gained nothing and lost nothing. Because you gain nothing, God alone benefits and thereby gets all the glory. The power of God is demonstrated and His testimony is honored.

Manifold possibilities poured into my mind. Why not pray Hannah's prayer daily? Why not prove God's power with the prayer of Hannah? I decided to do just that: Prove God's power with the prayer of Hannah. I would ask God for something specific that I would not otherwise expect to acquire. Upon receiving that which He would give, I would return it to Him.

Why not prove God's power with the prayer of Hannah?

By now my office was illuminated with the first rays of dawn. As the sun cleared the horizon, I took my Bible and again read Hannah's prayer. When I knelt to pray that morning, I prayed with a renewed sense of urgency. "God give me something I can give back to You." I wasn't quite sure what to ask for until later that evening.

☙ APPLYING THE PRINCIPLE

After supper I left home to attend a board meeting at church. Some years earlier the congregation had borrowed money to erect a small multi-purpose building. Now the mortgage was placing considerable strain on our little church's budget. Under the leadership of our pastor, the congregation vowed never again to borrow money. That, however, didn't remove the burden of making monthly payments.

We considered our options. Should we try to sell the building? Perhaps we could rent it?

Asking for more money from our people was not an option. They were already giving sacrificially.

How, then, could we meet our obligations?

"What about Hannah's prayer?" I asked.

Together we turned to I Samuel chapter 1 and reviewed her words. *O LORD of hosts, if thou wilt indeed look on the affliction of thine handmaid, and remember me, and not forget thine handmaid, but wilt give unto thine handmaid a man child, then I will give him unto the LORD all the days of his life.*[1]

The board agreed to ask God for money to give back to Him. "O Lord of hosts," we prayed, "if you will indeed look on the affliction of your church, and remember it, and not forsake it, but if you will give us funds from unexpected sources in addition to monies we're already receiving, then we will give those funds unto the LORD and vow to stay out of debt." *We prayed. God responded.*

The next Sunday our Pastor called upon the congregation to pray Hannah's prayer. We prayed. God responded. The course of our little church was changed.

The very next day, I received notice from my long-distance phone carrier that my rates were being reduced. (When was the last time that happened to you?) At first, I thought little of it. The total savings would be only five dollars per month or about $60 dollars that year.

17

Then it occurred to me. That's $60 I would not have received otherwise. Is this an answer to Hannah's prayer? The next Sunday I wrote a check for $60, marked it "Hannah money," and placed it in the offering plate.

Shortly thereafter a young woman spoke up during a testimony service. After praying the Hannah prayer, she found twenty-five dollars near her pillow. She had no idea how it got there. None of her family knew either. Apparently, she had tucked it away some time ago for safekeeping. She then forgot about it until it fell from its hiding place. Here was money from an unexpected source. She called it "Hannah money" and gave it to the church. The mortgage was reduced by exactly twenty-five dollars.

Another person received a $1,200 income tax refund unexpectedly.

A businessman testified to getting a notice from a supplier who had been over charging him. The supplier sent about $1,500 to balance the account. That was money unexpected. The mortgage dropped again.

One lady was joyous over getting an un-unexpected discount while shopping. "My first thought was to treat myself to lunch," she testified. "But the Lord seemed to tell me, 'this is Hannah money.'" The mortgage fell yet again.

A boy found $5 in a grocery store. He gave it to the store manager. The manager gave it back. The mortgage decreased another $5.

There are many other test-imonies of God supernaturally responding to the prayer of Hannah. And the story goes on.

There is no limit to what God can do through you.

This is the principle behind Hannah's prayer. Right now, consider praying the prayer of Hannah. Ask God for something that will enhance His testimony. Ask Him for something that you can give back to Him. Always be mindful that you serve a big God. There is no limit to what He can do through you.

Consider this prayer: "O LORD of hosts, if you will indeed look on my affliction and remember me, and not forget me, but provide that which I can give back to you, then I will, indeed, surrender it fully to your glory. Amen."

Before you pray, I urge you to read I Samuel chapters 1 and 2. Note how God honored Hannah. More importantly you will discover that Hannah possessed eight important character qualities. These traits allowed God to use her mightily. They are outlined in the next eight chapters of this book. As you read, you will learn how you, too, can effectively pray the prayer of Hannah!

Let's get started...

1. I Samuel 1:11
2. I Samuel 1:20

Chapter 2

Hannah's Humility

Imagine sitting by the Sea of Galilee. Jesus is there with you. Together you are enjoying a casual time of fellowship while feasting on a breakfast of fresh fish. A brief moment of silence punctuates the conversation. You look at Jesus. He seems to be gazing into the distance as if in deep contemplation.

Then, in a serious but mellow tone, He abruptly asks, *"Lovest thou me more than these?"*

There's another moment of silence. You're not sure how to answer. Still, His eyes seem fixed on some point far into the sea.

Lovest thou me more than what? you wonder.

Then it dawns on you. He's looking at your net full of fish. Last night He commanded you to cast your net on the other side of the boat, which you did. Amazingly, your net was so full of fish that it took you, Nathaniel, Thomas, James, John, and two others to lug it to shore.

One-hundred-fifty-three big fish, you think. You know. You counted them. That's more than a full month's salary. Not bad for one night. Let's see, what was the question again?

"Lovest thou me more than these."

"Yes, Lord," you reply. "You know that I love you."

"Feed my lambs," He adds quietly.

You're still thinking about the fish.

I wonder if I can do it again tomorrow? you ask yourself. Enough catches like this and I can retire!

You notice the net hasn't broken.[1] That's a good sign.

Jesus interrupts your thoughts. He calls you by name and asks a little more firmly, *"Lovest thou me?"*

"Yes, Lord," you answer again. "You know that I love you."

Maybe James and John will come back and help again. In fact, if this keeps up, you think, I'll need to hire some help, probably need to buy a bigger boat, upgrade my nets, and…

"Lovest thou me?" This time there's a sense of urgency in His voice. He's almost shouting.

"Lord, you know everything; you know that I love you!"

You look into His eyes. He looks into yours. He smiles, raises His eyebrows, and quietly yet resolutely repeats, *"Feed my sheep."*

You are Simon Peter. You've just been asked to relinquish a windfall profit, a respectable career and financial security. Three years ago He called you to be a fisher of men. Now, He's enlarging your ministry. He's calling you to be a shepherd of men as well. You're being asked to give up everything that is important to you to take up everything that's important to Him.[2]

You're being asked to give up everything that is important to you.

That morning Peter not only walked away from his windfall profit, career and security. He walked away from his self-will. And what did he get in their place?

A few days later he was passing by the Temple in Jerusalem. A lame beggar asked for some loose change. Peter was penniless. He left his profit potential on Galilee's shore.

"Silver and gold have I none," he told the lame man. "But I don't mind giving you what I do have."

What Peter had was far more valuable than anything that poor beggar could have expected and certainly worth more than 153 fish.

"In the name of Jesus Christ of Nazareth, rise up and walk." And walk he did. And leap. And praise God.

ଔ THE PRINCIPLE OF SURRENDER

Peter's transformation is a picture of humility. It is giving up "these" so God can use you mightily. To Peter, "these" meant his career. To Hannah "these" referred to her single greatest desire, a son. Humility is the starting point where the power of God is made manifest in your life, not occasionally, but routinely. *Humility is willfully surrendering one's will.*

To understand the dynamic of humility, reconsider Jesus staring at Peter's catch and asking, "Lovest thou me more than these?" Then, imagine Jesus is with you, personally, right now. He is asking you *"Lovest thou me more than these?"* as He gazes at those things that are most important to you.

At what things is He staring? Your career? Your security? Your family? Your health? Your reputation?

What is your answer?

Will you simply say, "Well, of course I love You! But more than these? Oh, I don't know about that. But you know, Lord, I do love You"?

Or will you sincerely answer, "Yes! I love you more than these"?

To love Jesus more than "these" is to stand on the threshold of experiencing the dynamic of Hannah's humility.

❧ LOOK BEFORE YOU LEAP

The fact that you are reading this little book strongly suggests that you, too, are searching for

God's best for your life. Can you identify with Hannah? Do you frequently cry out to God for His blessings?

Together, we'll explore the spiritual dynamics that empowered her. As you read, you will also discover her secret to moving the *God uses* hand of God. When you do, keep *ordinary* this in mind: The omnipotent God *people* who delighted in answering the *like you.* prayer of Hannah is *your* God. He has not changed. As God responded to her, He will respond to you.

God uses ordinary, humble[3] people, like you, who choose to willfully surrender their will and—with absolute dependence on Him—step out on faith.

When Peter walked away from the Galilean shore that day, he began by taking one little step. Taking steps of faith was not new to Peter. He had trusted Jesus once before.

The wind was boisterous, and their tiny ship was subjected to the whim of the waves. It was late at night, and the disciples found themselves stranded in the middle of the Sea of Galilee. Jesus captured their undivided attention by walking to them on the water. Peter asked, *Lord, if it be thou, bid me come unto thee on the water.* Jesus said, *Come.* Peter came.[4]

Feeling the water's cool surface under his feet must have been an exhilarating experience for Peter. But his faith was truly enlarged when he began to sink! It wasn't until then that the frightened fisherman experienced the outreached hand of Jesus lifting him to safety. He learned that when the Lord invites you to step out on faith, you will never have cause to doubt.

❧ MISPLACED FAITH

Did you know that walking by faith is not always the will of God? Don't misunderstand. Let me assure you that we are to walk daily by faith. However, there is a type of faith that *honors* the Lord, and there is a type of faith that *dishonors* the Lord.

In your mind's eye, picture Peter standing on the edge of his boat ready to take a step of faith.

Peter did not take that first step until after he heard Jesus say, "Come."

Now, imagine Jesus standing on a pinnacle of the Temple. Satan says, "Jesus, take a step of faith! After all, God has promised to send His angels to catch you."[5] Jesus knew that such faith was *misplaced* faith.

It was the will of God for Peter to step off the side of his boat and trust the Lord to catch him. But it was *not* the will of God for Jesus to step off the pinnacle and expect the angels to bear Him up.

What was the difference?

ଝ T R U S T I N G   O R   T E M P T I N G ?

The answer is obvious: Peter was invited by the Lord—Jesus was summoned by Satan. The distinction, however, goes much further. It is the difference between *trusting* God and *tempting* God.

Jesus responded to Satan's enticement by saying, *Thou shalt not tempt the Lord thy God*. Peter was correct in trusting God, as Jesus was correct in refusing to tempt God.

Note the contrast between trusting and

tempting. Trusting God begins with a *humble, surrendered* spirit. Tempting God begins with a *willful, selfish* spirit. *Trusting* God responds to the clear leading of the Lord. *Tempting* God goes ahead of the Lord, then expects Him to catch us when we fail.

David understood this principle when he wrote, *the Lord is my Shepherd,* then added, *he leadeth me.*[6] David realized the role of the shepherd is to walk in front of the sheep. He knew the sheep patiently trust the shepherd's wisdom and follow him. They don't move until he moves. They don't tempt him by running ahead and expecting him to come along in due time. They wait until He says, "Come."

Trusting God begins with a humble, surrendered spirit.

David didn't rashly pursue the Philistines, then expect God to protect him. That would have been tempting God. Rather, *David enquired of the LORD, saying, Shall I go and smite these Philistines?* He waited until *the LORD said unto David, Go, and smite the Philistines, and save Keilah.*[7]

29

David waited for the Lord to say, "Go." Peter waited for Jesus to say, "Come." Likewise, Hannah humbly waited on the Lord. The essence of humility is doing God's work in God's way in God's time.[8]

Before you step out on faith, ask yourself this vital question: Am I humbly trusting God, or am I willfully tempting God? Remember, humility is willfully surrendering one's will.

∞ OPEN DOORS, CLOSED DOORS

Well-meaning Christians often presume that the will of God is determined by circumstances. "If God opens the door," they say, "I will go." Humility, however, is manifested when we submit to God's will regardless of circumstances.

A classic example of this principle is seen in the book of Acts.

In Acts 12 we find Peter imprisoned.

In Acts 16 we find Paul imprisoned.

In the Jerusalem jail where Peter was staying, the doors were miraculously opened.

In the Philippian jail where Paul was staying

the doors were also miraculously opened.

The similarities stop there. It was the will of God for Peter to walk through the doors of the Jerusalem jail. On the other hand, it was the will of God that Paul *not* walk through the doors of the Philippian jail. The fact that the doors were opened had no bearing whatsoever on the perfect will of God. Our desire should always be to do the will of God, when the doors are opened and when the doors are closed.

Our desire should always be to do the will of God.

Hannah's door was closed. As such, she could have reasoned that her barrenness was God's will. Rather, she sought the will of God *beyond* her circumstances. It was clear to her that the absence of blessings in her life was not the will of God.

Because she was not content with the few mercy drops falling around her, Hannah pleaded for showers of blessings. As a result of her humility, God did shower her with blessings. Not only did He give her a son, but blessed her with five additional children.[9] Hannah received more than she asked and more than she thought to ask.[10]

By willfully surrendering your will, you, too, can expect God's richest blessings. You will no longer sing "Mercy drops 'round us *are* falling," but "Mercy drops 'round us *were* falling. Now it's the showers we see!"

1. cf., Luke 5:6
2. John 21:1-19
3. I Corinthians 1:27
    James 4:67.
4. Matthew 14:22-33
5. Matthew 4:5-7
6. Psalm 23:1,2
7. 1 Samuel 23:2
8. Psalm 127:1
9. I Samuel 2:21
10. Ephesians 3:20

Chapter 3

Hannah's Brokenness

Todd and Tom were twin brothers. At age 19 they each made a career choice.

Todd decided to become a soldier. He willfully surrendered his will to the recruitment officer and was shortly thereafter assigned to a drill sergeant for rigorous training.

Tom, on the other hand, opted to be a bank robber. He willfully demanded cash at a local savings and loan and was shortly thereafter assigned to a prison guard for five years' hard labor. While Todd was enduring brokenness as a form of *preparation*, Tom was enduring brokenness as a form of *punishment*.

We see, then, there are two types of brokenness.

The first is *preparational brokenness*. It follows humility. Once the will is surrendered, the good soldier will endure hardship as he prepares for future duty.[1]

The second is *punitive brokenness*. It precedes humility. When the will is not surrendered, the offender is punished for his willful spirit until he becomes humble. (See Luke 15:18-21).

This parallels with the principle of trusting vs. tempting which we learned in the previous chapter.

When we humbly *trust* God, our submissive spirit positions us for preparational brokenness.

When we willfully *tempt* God, our selfish spirit positions us for punitive brokenness.[2]

Be careful not to confuse preparational brokenness with punitive brokenness. Notice Peter's warning. *Beloved, think it not strange concerning the fiery trial which is to try you,* he advised, *as though some strange thing happened unto you.*[3]

❧ THE AUTHOR OF CONFUSION

Over the years I have pastored, taught, and counseled hundreds of dedicated, humble Christian people. Nearly all of them were enduring some form of brokenness such as financial burdens, health problems, difficult relationships, or some other painful experiences. In most cases, they were not being punished by God. Rather they were enduring a process of preparation.

Many of these good folks, however, could not understand why God permitted their pain. Their lack of understanding was rooted in confusion. They confused preparational brokenness with punitive brokenness. They were convinced God was punishing them unjustly. In reality, God was preparing them for greater service.

In reality, God was preparing them for greater service.

Repeatedly, I heard such questions as, "Why would God allow this to happen to me when I have been serving Him faithfully?" They thought it strange that God would allow such fiery trials to beset them.

When we confuse preparational brokenness with punitive brokenness, we will always come to wrong conclusions. It causes us to determine that God is not meeting our needs, after all. We falsely assume God is not a just God. We see Him as an uncaring bully.

Such confusion is fertile soil for birthing a rebellious spirit. We turn away from God, His church, and His blessings. When we do, Satan has us exactly where he wants us.

The Apostle Paul, however, informed us that God is not the author of confusion.[4] Rather, he said, God has blessed us with the spirit of a sound mind.[5]

Have you willfully surrendered your will to the Lord?

Have you willfully surrendered your will to the Lord? If so, your adverse circumstances are not punitive, but preparational.

Peter said there is a need for these difficulties.[6] It is important that we understand— not only *what* God is doing when He prepares us—but also *why* He is doing it.

Preparational brokenness is your drill sergeant. Just as a soldier expects rigorous training, you should expect fiery trials. God purposely allows character-building circumstances to enter your life. Don't think it strange when these fiery trials arise as you faithfully serve the Lord. Think it strange when they *don't* arise.

Hannah's humility positioned her for preparational brokenness. Her experiences were her drill sergeant. They taught her the importance of depending on the Lord. God used Hannah mightily because she applied this principle. As a result of her broken spirit, God was glorified.

☙ GOD'S TESTIMONY AT STAKE

Two people played a vital role in Hannah's life. The first was Elkanah. He was Hannah's husband, friend and advocate. The second was Peninnah. This spiteful woman hated Hannah and caused her much sorrow.

Hannah longed for just one son. Though grateful for her few blessings, she determined to settle for nothing less than God's absolute best. *And she was in bitterness of soul, and prayed unto the LORD, and wept sore.*[7]

Elkanah tried to console his wife. *Am not I better to thee than ten sons?*[8] he asked.

Do you know people like Elkanah? They are

37

well meaning, but very often wrong. Sometimes good people give bad advice. Their purpose is support, but their effect is opposition.

Hannah didn't reply verbally, but her answer was obvious. "No, nothing is better than the full blessings of God." You'll discover the significance of her silence in chapter 8.

❧ CONSIDER GOD'S REPUTATION

Think of a time in your life when the blessings of God were not evident. During those arid seasons of the soul, how does the world respond?

"So," they say, "you're a Christian. Where is your God? We don't see Him. Maybe He doesn't care. Does He even exist? We certainly don't see Him working in your life."

Does it grieve you when God's blessings are absent in your life?

This was Hannah's dilemma. God's blessings were not evident. His reputation was questioned because His power was not seen.

When the full blessings of God are not apparent in our lives, the world takes note. They challenge the wisdom of living for the Lord. They compare their possessions with our meager blessings and, like Peninnah, conclude our God is powerless.

Peninnah was Elkanah's other wife. Blessed with children, she unceasingly mocked Hannah. Why? Because she did not see the power of God in Hannah's life. *And her adversary also provoked her sore, for to make her fret, because the LORD had shut up her womb.*[9]

Hannah's tears, then, transcended personal desires.

Peninnah thought she was only ridiculing Hannah. In reality, she was maligning God's reputation. She failed to recognize one very important fact: The God who withheld Hannah's blessing was also the God who could release her blessing. God was merely awaiting Hannah's prayer.

Hannah's tears, then, transcended personal desires. Protecting her reputation was a secondary concern. Most importantly, she sorrowed that God's testimony was challenged, and His faithfulness had been brought into question.

When the power of God is not abundantly evident in our lives, it also should break our hearts. The absence of God's blessings should compel us to pray the prayer of Hannah—not because we desire a blessing—but because we desire God's power be manifested and His testimony protected. When God is not demonstrating His power through us, there is something amiss. It's time to pray.

God wants to release His blessing in your life.

God wants to release His blessing in your life. He is patiently, yet eagerly, waiting in His "Oval Office" for you to pray the prayer of Hannah. James said it quite succinctly, *Ye have not because you ask not* ...[10]

We understand, then, the meaning of preparational brokenness. It is when God allows our hearts to be broken with the things that break His heart. It is when God allows adversity to strengthen us spiritually. God is prepared to pour out His blessings when we are willing to be broken. And, most importantly, it is that which turns our hearts to the Lord in prayer.

᠀ WEEDS AND SEEDS

A few summers ago I declared war on a weed patch in my backyard. Normally I don't mind perennials—but dandelions?

With shovel in hand, I laboriously turned the turf until every weed had disappeared. I then repeatedly spaded the ground as each bit of earth was broken into one fine, uniform layer of soil. It was time for the grass seed. Wanting to be sure any future weeds would have plenty of competition, I generously covered the patch with seeds, then raked it neatly and evenly. What was once a patch of weeds had become a blanket of seeds.

Just as I was completing the project, I noticed an ominous thundercloud approaching. When the first drops of rain fell, I rushed into the house to wait out the storm. Within fifteen minutes the tempest had passed and the sun was again shining.

Curiously, I returned to the newly created seed patch to see how it had weathered the storm. I was surprised to see the seeds had completely

41

disappeared. Where had they gone? The rain forced them deep into the soil! A few weeks passed. What was once infested with weeds was now teeming with beautiful green grass.

The spiritual implications are obvious. Your life is the patch of ground. It's overrun with weeds of self-willfulness.

• Breaking the soil is punitive brokenness that destroys the weeds of selfishness. If the soil of your heart is not broken, the seeds of God's Word will not take root.

• Planting the seed is humility, when the Word of God is selflessly accepted. If the soil is broken, but not seeded, the breaking process will be in vain. It will only produce more weeds of self-willfulness.

• The storm is preparational brokenness, through which His Word takes root deep in our hearts. If there is no storm, the seeds will not penetrate the broken soil, and the breaking and seeding processes will be in vain.

We see, then, that God allows punitive brokenness for two reasons. *First*, to destroy the weeds of selfishness rooted in the soil of your heart. *Second*, to allow storms of adversity to force the seed of His Word deep into that soil. There it takes root, grows, and bears evidence of His presence. It is the combination of broken hearts, the Word of God, and adversity that makes us usable to God.

Confident that her trials were not punishment, Hannah was able to boldly approach the throne room of God. You, too, can seek the face of God with that same confidence. And there's more! In the following chapter, you will learn how a humble, broken spirit will allow you to see God's purpose for your life by obtaining His perspective.

Ask not what God can do for you. Ask what God will do through you.

1. II Timothy 2:3
2. Hebrews 12:6
3. I Peter 4:12
4. I Corinthians 14:33
5. II Timothy 1:723
6. I Peter 1:6
7. I Samuel 1:10
8. I Samuel 1:8
9. I Samuel 1:6
10. James 4:2

Chapter 4

Hannah's Meekness

In another day and time, they would have been called street urchins. Without restraint they ran among the throngs that crowded the downtown sidewalks. It seemed like such fun, and I was missing the excitement. I envied their freedom, desiring to tag along as they lost themselves in the sea of people.

Getting lost, however, was not an option. My father held a firm grip on my small hand as my four-year-old legs scurried to keep pace with his long strides.

This was Indianapolis, 1957.

Within a few days, some 400,000 race fans would converge on our city. Many had already arrived. They were mingling with the crowd of local residents who had come to see the Memorial Day Parade, or Race Day Parade as they call it in Indy.

The festivities were about to begin.

The faint sound of Elvis crooning from someone's car radio could be heard above the crowd. The sweet smell of cotton candy tempted my senses as it blended with the aroma of steaming hot dogs. I longed to break free and satiate my curiosity. I wanted to be one of the urchins.

From a 4-year-old's perspective, my father's grip seemed painfully pointless. He, of course, knew better. He was acutely aware of the dangers that lurked beneath the surface of my childish desires. As a youngster, my father endured similar temptations.[1] His hold was, in reality, a simple act of love born of the wisdom that comes from experience.

He had brought me here for a purpose, to see the parade.

After all, he had brought me here for a purpose, to see the parade. I still wasn't interested. I had never seen a parade before and had no idea what it was all about. I *had* spied an ice-cream vendor, however. I would readily exchange all the parades in the world for one lick of creamy chocolate any day. That opinion was about to change.

Ignoring my constant tugging and pointing, my father led me to a convenient place near a curb. From this vantage point, he could see over the crowd and have full view of the coming procession. There we stood in silent anticipation. Of what? I didn't know.

Somewhere down the street we heard the rhythmic beat of a marching band. It caught the attention of my curious young mind. The closer the drumming drew, the greater my curiosity became. There was something going on, and I didn't want to miss it for the world.[2]

By the time the band reached us, Elvis was drowned out by the band's brass section and its earsplitting rendition of *Back Home Again In Indiana*. I wanted to see what my father was seeing, but my short stature limited my vision to the belt buckles and waistlines of the other onlookers.

By peeking between a lamp post and a mailbox, I caught a glimpse of marching legs, dressed in starched red trousers and stepping in perfect time, line after line. I wanted more than just a glimpse.[3] I wouldn't be satisfied until I saw it all.

I tugged my father's sleeve to get his attention. He immediately looked down when I reached up. His strong arms hoisted me above his head then set me on his powerful shoulders.

From there I caught my first glimpse of a majorette. I wrapped my arms around my father's head and buried my chin in his thinning hair. The majorette flung her baton high into the air. I fully expected it to fall back to earth

He immediately looked down when I reached up.

and whack her on the head. It didn't. She twirled, caught her baton, and high-stepped down the street with her band close behind.

The band was followed by dazzling floats, clowns and the Indianapolis Police Department's Motorcycle Drill Team. Most memorable, however, were the cowboys on horseback. The sight of their stately steeds clopping along the pavement shed a whole new light on Roy Rogers,

Zorro, and the Cisco Kid. The words "Hi ho, Silver" would forever have new meaning.

My previous desires proved no match for marching bands, waving celebrities and the Mercury Turnpike Cruiser pace car. It's amazing the difference a few moments can make. I had totally forgotten the urchins and their ice cream.

Once on my father's shoulders, I gained a new perspective. I gained his perspective. Those old desires passed away and were replaced with new desires.[4]

❧ UNDER GOD'S CONTROL

Like a youngster discovering for the first time what the parade is all about, one who is captured by meekness learns God's true purpose for life. It causes the heart to ponder the meaning of one's existence, tug on the Father's sleeve for an answer and be lifted to His shoulders for a clear view.

Meekness is a spiritual condition that compels us to crave the things of God more than the things of the world. With it, we are no longer content to follow along in our own wisdom. Rather, when we are meek, we willingly relinquish our strength to rely fully on the Heavenly Father.

Meekness, by definition, is *human strength under God's control.*[5] It enriches our faith to create an indefatigable dynamic that has driven history's most effective spiritual giants.

The prayer of Hannah is a classic example. She had caught a glimpse of God's blessings. Then, comparing her old desires to the Father's perspective, Hannah realized she was missing something big. She set aside her own wisdom and consciously abandoned the natural to trust God for the

From that lofty height, she experienced the Father's perspective.

supernatural. She boldly stepped into the throne room of God, lifted her arms to her heavenly Father, and surrendered. From that lofty height, she experienced the Father's perspective. She saw the parade.

Faith enriched by meekness gave Noah the courageous tenacity to not only stand alone, but thrive under the pressures of ridicule and rejection[6]. It was meekness that emboldened Gideon to fear God rather than men and free his people from the Midianites' oppression.[7] In the spirit of Gideon's meekness, Peter and John withstood the Sanhedrin and openly proclaimed the Gospel to the dying masses.[8]

Meekness is seen in the Apostle Paul crying from a shroud of darkness, *"Lord, what wilt thou have me to do?"*[9]

What God had the apostle to do altered the course of human history.

The God of Hannah, Noah, Gideon, Peter, John, Paul, and a myriad of other champions of faith[10] is your God. What would He have you to do?

❧ THE GIFTS OF GRACE

Again, meekness is defined as human strength under God's control.

Once lifted to your Heavenly Father's shoulders, your abilities submit to His will. Your limited strengths are exchanged for His abundant strengths. You become meek. Meekness, therefore, does not make you weak; it makes you spiritually strong. Each strength is a blessing, or grace gift, from God. Because these grace gifts are blessings that come in the form of God's strength, I have chosen to call them *blessing-strengths*. There are at least six of them.

• The first blessing-strength is *entering into the Father's rest.*[11]

You are no longer making the effort. You cease from your own labor to become His work. He makes the effort. As you patiently rest on your Father's shoulders, your tiny spiritual legs are replaced with His infinite strength.

You cease from your own labor to become His work.

With your renewed strength, you will likely find yourself doing far more for the Lord than you previously imagined possible. The meek *shall renew their strength; they shall mount up with wings as eagles; they shall run, and not be weary; and they shall walk, and not faint.*[12]

51

Such strength is not natural. It is spiritual. It comes from dependence on His abilities—alone.

• The second blessing-strength is *obtaining the Father's direction*.

When the Father moves, you move. When the Father turns, you turn with Him. Ruth captured the essence of this grace gift. To Naomi she said, *whither thou goest, I will go; and where thou lodgest, I will lodge: thy people shall be my people, and thy God my God.*[13]

Solomon understood this principle as flowing from the wellspring of godly wisdom. *I have taught thee in the way of wisdom;* He wrote, *I have led thee in right paths. When thou goest, thy steps shall not be straitened; and when thou runnest, thou shalt not stumble.*[14]

• The third blessing-strength is *gaining the Father's perspective*.

Hannah realized that God is glorified when He answers prayer.[15] Therefore, she refused to accept her barrenness. She chose instead to allow God to glorify Himself through her by giving her a son.

Likewise, we should refuse to accept our spiritual barrenness. As we peek through the crowd, we see there is more to life than the pleasures of the world, much more! Therefore, we cry out to God for the full view that can only be seen from His shoulders. Like Hannah we pray *look on the affliction of thine handmaid, and remember me.*[16] He will give us His perspective. We, too, will see the parade.

...meekness offers freedom from the consequences of sin

• The fourth blessing-strength is *acquiring your Father's protection.*[17]

Like lost urchins, there are many who choose to enjoy the pleasures of this world for a season.[18] They relish their freedom from restraint. They pity the children who are resting on their Fathers' shoulders, often deriding them for their foolishness.

Unfortunately, the god of this world has blinded his children to the ever present dangers that accompany self-willfulness.[19] While worldliness offers freedom from restraint, meekness offers freedom from the consequences of sin.[20] Worldliness craves temporary pleasures. Meekness sets its affection on eternity.[21]

• The fifth blessing-strength is *having access to your Father's provisions*.

The Syrophoenician woman asked for nothing more than a crumb from the Master's table. As a result of her faith, her daughter was delivered from demonic oppression.[22] Consider this: If one small crumb can provide such tremendous results, imagine what power will be manifested in the whole loaf of bread!

...imagine what power will be manifested in the whole loaf of bread!

Hannah acknowledged the unlimited storehouse from which her provisions came. She prayed, *for the pillars of the earth are the LORD's, and he hath set the world upon them.*[23]

Notice, also, Hannah's understanding of the blessing-strengths of meekness. She added, *He will keep the feet of his saints, and the wicked shall be silent in darkness; for by strength shall no man prevail.*[24]

• The sixth blessing-strength is *receiving the desires of the Father.* The following chapter is dedicated exclusively to this grace gift.

1. Hebrews 4:15
2. I John 2:15
3. I Corinthians 2:9
4. II Corinthians 5:15-17
5. Bill Gothard, *The Sevenfold Power of First-Century Churches and Homes,*
   Institute in Basic Life Principles, 2000, page 66
6. Genesis 6-9
7. Judges 6,7
8. Acts 4:19,20
9. Acts 9:6

10. Hebrews 12:1
11. Hebrews 4:10
12. Isaiah 40:31
13. Ruth 1:16
14. Proverbs 4:12
15. John 14:13
16. I Samuel 1:11
17. Leviticus 25:18

18. Hebrews 11:25
19. II Corinthians 4:4
20. Romans 6:20-22
21. John 8:35,36
22. Mark 7:28,29
23. I Samuel 2:8
24. I Samuel 2:9

Chapter 5

Hannah's Desire

"A cheeseburger sounds good right about now."

And so I hop in my '62 Chevy and speed through the darkened, rain-soaked streets toward Burger Chef.

Three myths are soon to be forever dismissed from my developing teen-age mind.

Myth No. 1: I learn that bright red, eight-sided signs bearing the reflective white letters S,T,O and P are not optional, even if I didn't see any other vehicles approaching.

Myth No. 2: Forever dismissed is that absurd notion, strangely held by some teen-age drivers, that they are somehow invisible to police officers.

The third myth is dispelled as I slowly pull to a stop at the side of the road and gaze into the rear-view mirror. With a lump in my throat and a shiver up my spine, my eyes betray a tinge of fear as they blink in perfect time with my thumping heart. I am awestruck as the silhouette of a husky thirty-something police officer emerges from a misty haze of headlamps and flashing red lights. As the rain-dampened, scowling officer beams his flashlight through my window, the third myth sinks forever into this sea of reality: Not everyone is cheerful during the Christmas season.

The officer patiently stands in the cold, December drizzle as I thumb through my wallet in search of my driver's license. I squint into the flashing lights while hoping my parents don't drive by.

"So, Mr. ... is it Jividen?" the officer queries.

"No, sir." I reply, "It's Gividen, like dividend, only it starts with a 'G'."

"So, Kenneth," the officer continues, "where do you attend high school?"

"Tech," I admit with some embarrassment. This isn't exactly a stellar year for our basketball team, and in the early 1970s that *is* important in Indiana!

"Do they teach you anything at Tech High School?" he rudely demands.

How does one answer that? And why do I feel as though this guy holds my life in the palm of his hand?

"Do they teach you how to read?" the officer continues. "Do you *know* that S,T,O and P are letters? Do you *understand* their meaning? And when you see those letters, do you take the *wise* course of action and come to a complete stop?"

I wipe the rain from my brow with my coat sleeve (there's a hole in the convertible roof) while the officer thrusts my driver's license back through the window. After a stiff warning about being careful and the dangers of injuring someone just before the holidays, the officer disappears back into the aura of flashing red lights.

Is it the cold rain, his fatherly compassion, or a very unusual Christmas gift? Or maybe all of the above? I can't help but wonder why. The police cruiser vanishes into the night without so much as a written warning.

Later, I will discover the officer's true gift was a powerful spiritual insight that I will cherish the rest of my life.[1]

❧ THE DESIRE TO PRAY

At first reading, you may get the impression that Hannah's prayer was born of her distress. But continue reading. In I Samuel chapter 2, we discover that once Hannah's prayer was answered—and after her heartache had turned to joy—Hannah continued to pray![2]

She prayed when distressed.

She prayed when rejoicing.

We see, then, that Hannah prayed without ceasing. She prayed when distressed. She prayed when rejoicing.

What was the secret to Hannah's desire for prayer?

Perhaps it was the same as Martin Luther, who desired to begin each day on his knees before God—sometimes for hours at a time.

The great reformer, John Knox—of whom Mary, Queen of Scots declared, "I fear the prayers of John Knox more than all the assembled armies of Europe" —possessed that desire.

The 18th century missionary, David Brainerd, desired to spend long sessions alone with God in the American wilderness. George Mueller's desire for prayer earned him a place as one of the 19th century's most effective Christians.

The Apostle Paul is another example. Not only did he challenge us to *pray without ceasing*, he revealed the catalyst that would propel the desire to do so. From his earliest days as a Christian,[3] Paul aspired to *know spiritual truth*. That desire is expressed in his letter to the Philippians, *That I may know him, and the power of his resurrection.*[4]

Like the police officer, Paul understood the value of of knowledge. He knew that *godly knowledge* precedes *godly understanding*,[5] which is the source for *godly wisdom*. Godly knowledge, understanding and wisdom—in turn—produce godly desire. Let me explain.

✿ GAINING UNDERSTANDING

S, T, O and P, along with 22 others, were letters I learned from my older sister long before I started school. I knew they were letters, but I had no concept of their meaning. I had *knowledge* but not *understanding*.

With the help of a first-grade reading circle and a dedicated teacher, I graduated from the *knowledge* of letters to *understanding* their meaning.

"See Spot run?" we would read. "Run, Spot, run."

Note that the four letters which spell *Spot* also spell *stop*. In addition, they spell *tops* and *pots*.

Simply knowing the letters is obviously insufficient. How would you understand the need to stop at the sign? It could be a spot sign!

The spiritual application, of course, is that without spiritual knowledge, there can be no spiritual understanding.

But what about wisdom?

⊂⊃ APPLYING WISDOM

Wisdom is the application of the understanding that comes from knowledge. I know S, T, O and P are letters. I understand their meaning: I am supposed to stop. But do I stop? It depends on whether or not I *apply* wisdom.

It is one thing to know and understand biblical truths. But merely possessing godly knowledge and understanding does not make us wise. It is not until we apply those truths that we exhibit true wisdom.

Jesus illustrated this principle by comparing a foolish man, who built his house on the sand and a wise man who built his house upon the rock. In this story, Jesus said the wise man came to Him (*knew* Him), heard His sayings (*understood* Him), and did the things which He said (applied *wisdom*).

...wisdom is something you do.

The foolish man, on the other hand, is described as one that *heareth, and doeth not.* In other words, the foolish man also had knowledge and understanding. Yet he failed to apply wisdom.[6]

Precisely stated, wisdom is something you do. It is the action of applying knowledge and understanding.

Building a house on a sure foundation is an action. It is something you wisely do. Stopping at a stop sign is also an action. It is something you wisely do. Praying is an action. It is something you wisely do.

Hannah clearly understood the relationship between knowledge and actions. She prayed, *for the LORD is a God of knowledge, and by him actions are weighed.*[7]

०२ DEVELOPING DESIRE

Spiritual knowledge, understanding, and wisdom comprise a three-tiered stairway that leads to godly desire. This stairway includes these four insights:

• The first insight is that *the application of godly wisdom nurtures a godly appetite.*

Hannah applied godly wisdom when she asked the Lord to give her that which she could give back to Him. Her later rejoicing was evidence of a cultivated desire for the things of the Lord.[8]

We, too, will taste the goodness of the Lord when we apply wisdom. We will then acquire a greater appetite for its goodness.[9]

Once we see the parade from the father's perspective, we want to stay on His shoulders. That is to say, once we see the evidence of effective praying, we desire to pray without ceasing. This was Hannah's secret.

• The second insight is this: *Increased godly desire will hunger for additional godly knowledge.*

As we experience the blessings of walking in wisdom, our spiritual man will desire *more* godly knowledge, resulting in greater understanding and wisdom. It is not a cycle, but a spiritual, spiral stairway.

Perhaps this is what the Apostle Paul had in mind when he wrote of growing from faith to faith,[10] thrilled at the unsearchable riches of God's wisdom and knowledge,[11] and challenged us to continually *walk by the same rule* and *mind the same thing.*[12] He later compared physical growth to growing in understanding.[13]

• Although this stairway has no end, *it does have a beginning.* This is the third insight.

Solomon identified that beginning. *The fear of the LORD,* he wrote, *is the beginning of wisdom: and the knowledge of the holy is understanding.*[14]

To fear the Lord—which is the beginning of wisdom—one must first know that He exist. Or, as the writer of Hebrews explains, *he that cometh to God must believe that he is.* Those who "know" there is no God, cannot fear Him and cannot, therefore, have godly wisdom. Their atheistic "knowledge" results in ungodly understanding which, in turn, leads to foolish actions. This brings us to...

• ...the fourth insight: *The absence of godly desire indicates foolishness.*

There are those who fail to understand why we desire to remain on the Father's shoulders.

They perceive our wisdom as foolishness[15] and their foolishness as wisdom. Why? Because they "know" there is no God. Our meekness appears to be weakness. Paul said they simply cannot understand because they are void of spiritual discernment.[16] They are on another staircase that is spiraling *downward*.

The first stairway begins with the fear of the Lord and produces godly desire.[17] The other begins *without* the fear of the Lord and—is not only void of godly desire—but is repulsed by it. Each step downward produces more *un*godly understanding and foolishness. Paul describes this progression in Romans 1:21-31. It's end, he said, is destruction.[18]

Our lack of desire for the things of the Lord—specifically prayer—should sound an alarm in our hearts. It indicates that we are on the downward stairway. Our fear of the Lord has waned, and the godly desire demonstrated by Hannah is absent from our lives.

So far—through training in the four disciplines of humility, brokenness, meekness, and desire—we have seen Hannah's character *development*.

In the following chapters, we will discover the *demonstration* of four additional disciplines of godly character.

We begin in a small Midwestern church.

1. Hebrews 13:2
2. II Samuel 2:1
3. Acts 9:18,19
4. Philippians 3:10
5. Colossians 1:9
6. Luke 6:46-49
7. I Samuel 2:3
8. I Samuel 2:1
9. Psalm 34:8
10. Romans 1:17
11. Romans 11:33
12. Philippians 3:16
13. I Corinthians 14:20
14. Proverbs 9:10
15. I Corinthians 1:21
16. I Corinthians 2:14
17. Proverbs 9:9
18. Philippians 3:19

Chapter 6

Hannah's Mercy

Preaching to small congregations always has been my passion. At one such church, I was pleased to discover the front row filled with students from a local Bible college.

"How many of you are Christians?" I asked.

They all raised their hands.

I elaborated. "If you were to be labeled—I mean, literally *labeled*—would the word 'Christian' accurately describe what is in you?"

Blank stares make a preacher nervous. They didn't quite understand my question. I tried to think of a way to explain.

Earlier that morning I had stopped by a fast food restaurant for breakfast. I still had a ketchup packet in my suit pocket. So, showing them the little red container labeled "ketchup," I rephrased the question.

"Does the word 'ketchup' accurately describe what is in this packet?"

More blank stares.

I wondered if I was getting through. At least I had their attention.

"Suppose the ketchup factory made a mistake. Suppose they placed ketchup in the mustard packets. Then, suppose they filled the packets labeled 'ketchup' with mustard? What is in this packet?"

"Dunno," one co-ed finally offered.

At last! A response. Well, that's better than a stare, I thought.

"So, how can we determine the true contents of the packet?" I continued.

She donned an impish grin. "Why don't you squeeze it and see what comes out?"

The student didn't realize it at the time, but she was making a powerful spiritual application.

The packet is supposed to be filled with ketchup. That's what the label indicates. The only way to know for sure is to squeeze it and see what comes out.

By analogy, Christians are supposed to be filled with mercy and other character qualities.

That's what the label "Christian" indicates. And one certain way to discover the true contents of our "packets" is to squeeze us.

Joseph was squeezed under the pressure of family rejection and, later, false accusations. The Apostle Paul was squeezed under the pressures of poor health and imprisonment.

Hannah was squeezed under the pressure of her barrenness. Elkanah, Peninnah and Eli added further pressure. What came out of her was mercy!

When life's pressures squeeze you—when you are under stress—what comes out? The answer is, "Whatever is inside you."

And what *should* be inside you?

↻ THE MIND OF CHRIST

Paul answered that question forthrightly when writing to the church in Philippi. *Let this mind be in you*, he wrote, *which was also in Christ Jesus.*[1] If the label reads "Christian" the contents should be *the mind of Christ*.

That, in turn, raises yet another question: What is the mind of Christ?

The mind of Christ, according to Paul, is to abandon one's reputation to become a servant.

It comes as a shock to some Christians that, like Christ, we are not to be concerned about our reputations. Typically, someone will ask, "What about my testimony?"

Our reputation is what others think about us. The resolution to this perceived dilemma is to understand that our *reputation* is not the same as our *character*. Our reputation is what others think about us. Our character—or testimony—is what God knows to be true of us, regardless of what others believe.

Remember the packet? We could say it had a reputation for being ketchup. But its true character wasn't known until it was squeezed.

Understanding the difference between *reputation* and *character* is so important that Jesus engaged His disciples in a conversation on this subject.[2]

He asked, *Whom do men say that I the Son of man am?* Jesus was asking, "What is My reputation?"

Or, "How have they labeled Me?"

To this the disciples replied, *Some say that thou art John the Baptist: some, Elias; and others, Jeremias, or one of the prophets.*

Notice this interesting insight: Jesus had gained a false reputation as being just another great preacher. Some thought He was no different from any other prophet. When Jesus is viewed merely as the "son of man," He is always misunderstood. Even today He has a reputation as being nothing more than a good person by those who know Him only as a man. *That was contrary to His reputation, but it was His true identity, His character.*

When asked, *But whom say ye that I am?* Peter declared, *Thou art the Christ, the Son of the living God.* He understood that Jesus was more than the son of man. He was also the Son of God. That was contrary to His reputation, but it was His true identity, His character.

Ask yourself, "Whom do men say that *I* am?" and "What labels have others placed on me?"

71

Like Hannah—whose brokenness was mistaken for drunkenness[3]—your reputation may also contradict your true character. Some may confuse your merciful spirit for mere human effort. Others may tarnish your reputation through false accusations, that is, false labels.

The vital question, then, is not, "Whom do men say that I am?" but "Who does God know that I am?" and "What is my true character?"

❧ MERCY THROUGH OMISSION

Mercy is a character trait that simply shows compassion. It is often a small act, but, like the proverbial mustard seed, can grow exponentially.

Sometimes mercy shows compassion through an *action*. And other times mercy shows compassion through *inaction*.

Hannah is an example.

Consider, for instance, Hannah's response when faced with opposition from three individuals: Elkanah, Peninnah and Eli, the priest.

What was her response to Elkanah's lack of empathy? Hannah could have mercilessly rebuked her husband for his insensitivity. Instead, she mercifully did not respond.[4]

In spite of Peninnah's provocations, Hannah did not render evil for evil. That inaction was an "act" of mercy. She chose, instead, to pray.[5]

Her encounter with Eli also revealed her merciful spirit. She respectfully explained her sorrow when he confused her passionate prayer for drunkenness. Rather than berate the elderly priest for his lack of insight, Hannah was merciful to Eli.[3] Hannah's merciful spirit was revealed by what she *didn't* do. It was an outward revelation of her inner spirit.

It was an outward revelation of her inner spirit.

The Bible is replete with other examples of God using outward pressures to reveal one's inner spirit. Job, Joseph and Paul each revealed godly character under duress.

Others failed the test.

Mercy is more than withholding a deserved punishment. It is frequently displayed through *acts of kindness.* Consider the following example.

ભ A SINGLE MUSTARD SEED

In broadcasting, market share is everything. The more listeners tune to a station, the more money advertisers are willing to spend. The key is to find an on-air personality who has the tenacity and raw talent to command a loyal audience.

At the end of the proverbial rainbow, there is, well, nothing.

Radio station WNAP found that personality in General Billy Patten. When he claimed the No. 1 ratings spot in his market, he was considered somewhat of a gold mine for his employer. Nationally, his peers recognized him as one of the top 10 disc jockeys in America. Locally, his knack for communicating captured the attention of tens of thousands of teen-agers.

Sitting on the pinnacle of success did wonders for Patten's paycheck. It did little for the emptiness in his soul and even less for his crumbling marriage. As a rock-music insider, Patten learned that parties and Porsches only go so far, and at the end of the proverbial rainbow, there is, well, nothing!

It was in this moment of depression and despair that mercy came his way. Literally.

Fielding phone calls and interacting with listeners was not unusual for the General. Patten loved talking to his fans. It's called "marketing prowess." A teen-ager would brag for weeks, maybe months, about his 30-second encounter with the famous disc jockey. One listener, however, took it a step further. Patten explains what happened:

"I was stranded in a snowstorm. Hearing I was snowbound, this teen picked me up and volunteered to take me to Indy from my home in Acton. While driving past his church, this angel of mercy popped the question, 'Will you come to church with me?' For two weeks I often thought about the invitation."

That simple invitation made a world of difference. Why? Because it was empowered by an act of mercy. When he finally attended, few at the church recognized him by his real name, Greg Patten. The Lord, of course, knew him well, and that night Greg would meet Him personally.

Shortly thereafter, he and his wife were baptized together and became active church members.

Today, the former "General" pastors the thriving Skyline Community Church in Fort Wayne, Indiana. He's heard nationally on his syndicated "Living In Today's World" radio program. All because of a simple, single act of selfless mercy.

❧ GIVING AND RECEIVING

"Give and it shall be given unto you!"

A country preacher's face turns beet red as he pounds the pulpit.

"If'n ya'll wanna git somethin' from the good and gracious Lord above, then y'all gonna have to start givin'. The way ta git," he adds, "is ta give."

"Amen, Brother!" the crowd responds.

Here we go again. Another sermon on money.

There's nothing wrong with that, I suppose. After all it *is* in the Bible. Then he throws us a curve.

The pastor challenges his congregation to look at the verses preceding Luke 6:38. And so we do.

"Now," he continues, "'xactly what is it the good Lord wants us to be givin' one 'nother?"

I'm amazed. Why hadn't I seen it before?

What we are to give, the preacher expounds, is gracious acts of kindness, love and mercy. But not a word about money. There it was in black and white—verses 31 through 37.

Over the years, I have heard scores of sermons that evoked Luke 6:38.

Give, and it shall be given unto you;
good measure, pressed down, and shaken together,
and running over, shall men give into your bosom.
For with the same measure that ye mete
withal it shall be measured to you again.

In each sermon, this passage was always presented as relating only to money. But, as this preacher explains, "It ain't gotta thing ta do with what's in yer pocket book. It's got everythin' ta do with what's in yer heart!"

And he's right!

Jesus said nothing in this passage about giving and receiving money. Rather, He taught that if we give compassionate mercy to others, He would bestow mercy on us. Why? Because our merciful spirit reflects that of the Father. Jesus said, *Be ye therefore merciful, as your Father also is merciful.*[6]

I wonder if this is why "the good and gracious Lord above" blessed Hannah? Could it be that the secret to Hannah's answered prayer included her merciful spirit?

The country preacher reveals the relationship between prayer and receiving mercy. He explains that God desires to shower us with unmerited forgiveness—that is, His mercy. What's more, God blesses us with unmerited favor—that is, His grace. This happens when we, like Hannah, *come boldly unto the throne of grace, that we may obtain mercy, and find grace to help in time of need.*[7]

1. Philippians 2:5
2. Matthew 16:13-17
3. I Samuel 1:13
4. I Samuel 1:8,9
5. I Samuel 1:6-10
6. Luke 6:36
7. Hebrews 4:16

Chapter 7

Hannah's Purity

Flickering torchlights danced with their own eerie shadows down cold, gray castle halls. Guards kept watch beneath a black, starless sky. The corridors failed to hear the echo of even one fainting footstep. Words quietly hid themselves behind quivering lips. No no one dared desecrate the silence. From deep within the bowels of that palatial home came the mournful wail of a weeping king, praying for the life of his newborn son. As the hours passed, the crying ceased. The king arose to weep no more. His son had died. God said, "No!"

If I regard iniquity in my heart, the psalmist later wrote, *the Lord will not hear me.*[1] Ask students of the Bible to identify an occasion when God declined to answer a prayer. Most frequently they will point to David's prayer for his infant son. The tragedy, of course, is that King David's own sin caused a righteous God to withhold His blessings.

The prayers of Hannah and David share this common theme: Both prayers concerned their sons. Hannah's prayer, however, was accepted while David's was rejected.

Why? Because Hannah's purity invited the hand of Almighty God to touch her barren womb, while David's prayer was clouded by sinfulness. Spiritual purity—defined as "the absence of sin in the presence of righteousness"—made the difference.

Purity is not being clean for the sake of cleanliness. It is being clean for the purpose of usefulness. Note the following illustration.

While preaching on the importance of purity, I asked the congregation to look through the wall and describe what they saw.

At first, the crowd looked a little puzzled. Then, realizing the principle being taught, they smiled as if to say, "Sorry, Kenn, we can't see through the wall."

One listener offered this simple, yet insightful, response. "You can't see through the wall because the wall is in the way!"

❧ OPAQUE CHRISTIANITY

The wall was opaque. Light could not pass through it. Therefore, you could not see through it.

A few Christians fail to have their prayers answered because they are spiritually opaque. The light of Christ cannot pass through them. They, themselves, are in the way.

The light of Christ cannot pass through them. They, themselves, are in the way.

Opaque Christians see little need for prayer.[2] They pray only when they are confronted with dire personal hardships. Even then, their prayers selfishly focus on their own discomforts.[3]

Allowing the glory of God to be seen through them is merely a cliché which, ironically, they sometimes use to draw attention to their own vain form of godliness.[4]

Though often wealthy in worldly goods, they are pathetically destitute in the things of the Lord.[5] Christ cannot truly be seen through them. The self-sufficiency of their tragic lives robs them of that blessing.

❧ T R A N S L U C E N T C H R I S T I A N I T Y

I then directed the congregation's attention to the rows of beautiful frosted windows that lined the auditorium. Because the windows were frosted, or translucent, they allowed light to pass through them. No clear image, however, could be seen. The windows, themselves, blocked the view.

Most Christians are spiritually translucent. They welcome the light of Christ flowing through them, but like beautiful stained glass, they want to share in the glory. They, too, want to be seen. As a result, Christ is not clearly manifested in their lives.

Translucent Christians tend to have feeble prayer lives. Because their prayers begin with their own convenience in mind, they are seldom answered.[6] Translucent Christians are typically sincere but spiritually immature. Often committed to the Lord, they are sensitive to the Holy Spirit working in their lives. If they continue to yield to His guidance, these baby Christians will flourish into radiant vehicles through which the power of God is routinely seen.

◌ TRANSPARENT CHRISTIANITY

One windowpane had been broken and replaced with clear glass. The congregation easily described the scene beyond this pane because it was transparent. The glass was there, but it could not be detected. It was invisible. There was nothing to block the view.

Like Hannah, they seek nothing for themselves, and everything for God.

Occasionally, you will find Christians who are spiritually transparent. Not only does the light of Christ flow through them, but His power is also clearly evident because they desire not to be seen. They want no glory for themselves. Rather, they pray that others would behold Christ through them as if they were clear glass.

The prayer of Hannah is a model prayer of transparent Christians. Like Hannah, they seek nothing for themselves and everything for God. Even when praying for personal needs, their pleas are driven by the desire to magnify the Lord through His mighty works.[7]

Transparent Christians are not concerned for their reputations nor do they offer prayers for their personal convenience. Rather, they are consumed with the daily challenge of allowing Jesus to be clearly seen through answers to their prayers. Their prayer lives exemplify this mandate: *He must increase, but I must decrease.*[8]

Such transparency was evident when Esther approached the throne of King Ahasuerus. Not fearing for her own life, she boldly appealed for the safety of her people. Like transparent glass, she was clear of selfish intent. Her personal welfare was not even a consideration. She said, *If I perish, I perish.*[9]

Transparency was seen in the life of Nehemiah, who selflessly yielded his personal ambition to benefit the work of the Lord. Through his dedication, the walls of Jerusalem were rebuilt, and the stage set for the return of the Jewish exiles from Babylonian captivity.[10]

It was also seen in the life of Moses, who willfully abandoned the security of Pharaoh's palace for the service of the King of Kings. The writer of Hebrews declared, *By faith he forsook Egypt, not fearing the wrath of the king: for he endured, as seeing him who is invisible.*[11]

❧ SEEING CHRIST THROUGH YOU

There are three areas of understanding which allow the Lord to distinctly shine through the lives of transparent Christians.

• First, transparent Christians are keenly aware of *the importance of purity.*

By reviewing Revelation 21:21 they realize that purity naturally produces transparency.

> *And the twelve gates were twelve pearls:*
> *every several gate was of one pearl:*
> *and the street of the city was pure gold,*
> *as it were transparent glass.*

The street mentioned by John in this passage is pure gold. In the absence of any impurities, that gold is transparent. Consequently, these people of God seek to remove the impurities of self-glory and unrighteousness in their lives so they may be as transparent as the those golden streets. Their desire is that nothing would cloud the character of Christ being seen through them.

• Second, transparent Christians understand *the purpose of prayer.*

Understanding the reason *why* we pray is essential to effective praying. Prayer's purpose is twofold: It is to *honor* and then *glorify* God. He is honored when we ask. He is glorified when He answers.

The prayers of transparent Christians are routinely answered because they recognize this objective. It is not to simply get an answer, but to glorify the Lord *in* the answer. They pray with this end in mind. When they pray, they ask not what God can do for them. Rather, they ask what God can do *through* them. Each prayer begins with the question, "How will this truly glorify the Lord?"

The prayer of Hannah is a classic example of such praying. Her end objective was not to obtain something for herself. It was to receive that which would glorify the Lord. He was honored when Hannah sought His help in her time of need. Rather than accept a life void of power, she committed her trials to Him.

She honored the Lord by asking Him to grant her request. The Lord was glorified by answering her prayer. Hannah understood that without an answer there is no glory. Had Hannah not prayed, she would have remained barren. God would not have been glorified.

Elijah is another example. He honored the Lord by asking for fire to fall from heaven and consume the altar of Baal. Had God not answered, He would not have been glorified.

You, too, are an example. You honor God by your prayers of faith. He is glorified when He answers.

• Third, transparent Christians understand *prayer's effect on people.*

Suppose a wealthy benefactor offered us access to $1 million. If we knew anyone in need, including ourselves, we could withdraw funds from the million-dollar account to meet those needs. We would welcome the opportunity to have a positive impact on the lives of others. No true Christians would ignore someone else's needs simply because they didn't want to be bothered with withdrawing funds. Or would they?

They were bothered with that which the Lord dearly loved.

The disciples were bothered when little children were brought to Jesus. He rebuked his inconsiderate followers, informing them that *such is the kingdom of God.*[12] Incredibly, therefore, the disciples were bothered with the kingdom of God! They were bothered with that which the Lord dearly loved.

Later, these same disciples were annoyed by the pleas of the Syrophoenician woman. Imagine their audacity in giving the Lord a direct order! *Send her away,* they demanded, *for she crieth after us.*[13] They were disturbed by her pleading and were unconcerned about her need. They didn't want to be bothered. Their convenience was more important than their compassion.

Transparent Christians don't mind being bothered with the things that concern the Lord. They are not inconvenienced by the necessity of praying for others. Transparent Christians do not hesitate to access the infinite wealth of the Benefactor on behalf of those in need. The cruelest thing they could do to others is fail to pray for them.

Likewise, your prayer life is affecting others right now!

They understand that it is the prayer of a *righteous* man that avails much.[14] Therefore, they place a tremendous priority on purity, realizing that others are affected by their prayers. They are sensitive to every smudge of sinfulness that would affect their prayers and, thereby, hinder the ones for whom they are praying.

Consider this important insight: The transparency of Esther, Nehemiah, and Moses touched the entire people of Israel. Likewise, your prayer life is affecting others *right now!* If you are praying for family members, for example, you are having a positive effect on them. If you are praying for those in your church, you are making a difference in their lives.

When you fail to pray for others, you are depriving them of the Benefactor's blessings. Samuel taught that failure to pray for others was sin! He wrote, *Moreover as for me, God forbid that I should sin against the LORD in ceasing to pray for you.*[15]

Samuel taught that failure to pray for others was sin!

Suppose Hannah had failed to pray. What negative impact would it have had on the nation of Israel? What if Samuel had never been born because Hannah didn't pray? The life of this powerful prophet coincided with the birth of Israel as a nation. His ministry laid a spiritual foundation that affected God's chosen people throughout their history. Had Hannah not prayed, his positive spiritual influence would never have been known.

Suppose you fail to pray. What negative repercussions will your prayerlessness have on those around you? What blessings are you robbing from those for whom you should pray? Remember, a prayer that is not offered cannot glorify God.

There are three perspectives from which we are viewed. We explored two of these in the previous chapter. The first was *how we are perceived by others.* We identified this as our reputation. The second was *how we are viewed by God.* This we called our character, or testimony. This is that "good name" which, King Solomon said, is to be chosen above great riches.[16] It is that which should be transparent.

In the next chapter we will investigate the third perspective: the biblical concept of self-perception—how we perceive ourselves—and its relationship to real inner peace.

1. Psalm 66:18

2. James 4:2

3. James 4:3

4. Colossians 2:18;
   II Timothy 3:5

5. Revelation 3:17

6. James 4:3

7. Psalm 70:4,5

8. John 3:30

9. Esther 4:16

10. Nehemiah 2:1-7

11. Hebrews 11:27

12. Luke 18:16

13. Matthew 15:23

14. James 5:16

15. I Samuel 12:23

16. Proverbs 22:1

Chapter 8

Hannah's Peace

There's something about the sobs of a broken-hearted 5-year-old that touches one's soul. Bobby's mother had dressed him in his Sunday best: a light blue suit, crisp white shirt and clip-on tie. By the time he leaped off the porch, ran down the sidewalk, and climbed into the church van, his shirttail was out. It wouldn't be long before the clip-on tie would go. Bobby fit right in with the other kids on board. Even Robert, the ten-year-old bully, wasn't picking on him.

After disembarking at church, Bobby was swept into the crowd, then vanished into his Sunday school class. His older sister and cousins usually looked after him, but today he was alone. He was the only black child in attendance.

There was nothing unusual about that Sunday to hold a place in my memory, other than Bobby's tears. Both Sunday school and the morning worship service were business as usual. After the final "amen", the adults engaged in friendly conversation. The "bus kids" collected their Bibles and Sunday school paraphernalia and headed to the van, except Bobby.

With his shirttail still out and his clip-on tie dangling from his jacket pocket, Bobby briefly arrested his sobs using his sleeve as a convenient hanky—never mind that he had one in his pocket. He just stood there, his little body heaving with every whimper, waiting for me to rescue him from his misery.

I pulled up a chair so we could be on eye level and gently pulled him close enough to hear his story.[1] I asked him why he was crying. His answer came in one simple word, "Robert!"

Recalling encounters with bullies from my school days, I imagined Bobby had been victimized by a push, pull, punch or perhaps had his Sunday school art project desecrated in some inhumane manner. As it turned out, it was none of the above. To Bobby, it was worse.

"Well," I inquired, "what did Robert do to you?"

Bobby's head was bowed and, with his little fist rubbing his teary eye, he mumbled, "He called me a ..." then blurted out the "n" word.

I blinked for a moment. My mind diligently searched for just the right words[2] to calm the little fellow's frustration. Before I could speak, Bobby added, "Robert doesn't like me because I'm black."

"No! That's not true!" I assured him. "Robert doesn't hate you because you're black."

"So why doesn't he like me?"

"Robert doesn't like you because he's a jerk!"

I was shocked that those words were coming from my own lips. Belittling Robert by calling him a jerk was not the best way to handle the situation. The point being made, however, was valid.

When Bobby said, "because I am," he was internalizing the blame.

When Bobby said, "because I am," he was internalizing the blame. Effectively, he was identifying himself as the cause for the verbal assault and heaping upon himself unjustified guilt for being who he was. In reality, Bobby was God's creation. Every unchangeable aspect of his being was God's handiwork. I could not allow him to believe anything less. I could not risk allowing him to spend the rest of his life accusing his Creator of designing him with an imagined inherent flaw.

By insisting "because he is", I returned the guilt to its rightful owner, namely, Robert. Robert was the one with the flaw, and it wasn't the work of his Creator. It was his own sinful nature.

Satan had lost the advantage of depriving this young person of a sense of personal dignity.

The bully had poked a hole in little Bobby's self esteem through which he was hemorrhaging a flood of self worth. A few more minutes of encouraging words[3] seemed to heal the emotional wound and helped Bobby deal with the trauma of being rejected by Robert.

Bobby rode home that Sunday with a renewed sense of worth. He was somebody because God had created him. His emotional storm, caused by Robert's rejection, was pacified. Satan had lost the advantage[4] of depriving this young person of a sense of personal dignity.

⍰ REJECTING OURSELVES

God has designed each of us with a healthy desire for a sense of personal worth. We need to know that we are loved, that we have value and that we have a place in the proverbial scheme of things. We long for the inner peace these things bring. I suspect this desire is part of God's plan to encourage us to seek Him,[5] for that sense of significance can only be realized by accepting ourselves as His workmanship.[6]

The Bible indicates that from the moment of our conception we are His design for His purpose.[7] This means every physical, emotional and intellectual fiber of our being is His craftsmanship. Our sense of worth is realized in accepting ourselves as His design. He is the potter. We are the clay. To not accept our design is to reject the Designer.[8]

Each of us has unchangeable features which appear to be flaws. In reality, those presumed "flaws" are God's marks of craftsmanship. They indicate our uniqueness and verify the existence of our divine purpose. They also encourage us to depend on Him.

I believe Satan's strategy[9] is to convince us that our value is limited to ourselves. When we fall for this lie, we exclude our true source of worth, which is our infinite Creator. Satan then points to our "flaws." He convinces us that we are less than God intended us to be.

We are further deceived into believing that our worth can be measured by comparing ourselves to others.[10] In doing so, we will inevitably fall short. We will think we are too young or too old; too tall or too short. We will believe we are the wrong color, have wrong features or that we are not quite smart enough. This inner conflict robs us of inner peace and surfaces as self-rejection. Like Bobby, we will find ourselves saying, "because I am."

❧ REJECTING OTHERS

Again, we are blinded to the unlimited worth we have in our Father. As a consequence, most people live their lives with a sense of emptiness, diligently searching for something to satisfy their desires for significance. Some confuse accumulating wealth with acquiring worth.[11] They assess their personal value in terms of possessions and the social standing they bring. Others base worth on personal achievement or recognition. Some believe it can be found in athletic abilities, social skills, physical appearance, intellect, musical gifts or some other talent.

We will feel inferior to some and superior to others. James called such thinking "evil."

Such humanistic thinking causes us to evaluate others as having greater or lesser significance. We may, therefore, feel inferior to those thought to have greater worth. Or, like Robert, we may become emotional bullies rejecting those who don't "measure up." Frequently we will do both. We will feel inferior to some and superior to others. James called such thinking "evil."[12]

This tragedy is compounded because, as a faulty basis for presuming worth, it will always fail. The intellectual will ultimately lose sharpness of the mind, the athlete is one accident away from losing his physique and the beauty will lose the advantage of youth. Eventually, we will reject everyone, including ourselves.

ଓ I N N E R   P E A C E ~ O U T E R   P E A C E

Hannah also understood that her value came from the Lord and not from the opinions of others. Do you remember her response when Eli, the temple priest, mistook her passionate praying for drunkenness? *No, my lord,* she replied, *I am a woman of a sorrowful spirit.*[13]

Hannah's three-fold response teaches us how to repel attempts to destroy[14] our sense of worth.

• First, she said "no!"

"No" is a powerful word. Hannah used it effectively. Essentially, she stated, "No, I am not what you said I am."

When you are tempted to believe your value is based on the opinions of others, simply resist[15] Satan's ploy by saying, "No! My worth is not determined by my gender, age, family history, intelligence, talents, appearance or any other unchangeable feature."

• Second, Hannah replaced the lie with the truth. Note her "I am" statement. She said, *I am a woman of sorrowful spirit.*

Merely denying the lie creates a void which can be filled with other lies. Therefore, replacing the lie with the truth is essential.[16]

Instead, the lie was replaced with the truth.

For example, once Bobby understood being black was not a fault, he could have replaced the first lie with another lie. He could have said, "Well, then, Robert must hate me because I'm only 5 years old."

Fortunately, this didn't happen. Instead, the lie was replaced with the truth.

This is the strategy Jesus used when tempted by the devil. He replaced Satanic lies with biblical truths.[17] There was no room for other lies.[18]

When denying the devil the opportunity to steal your worth, replace it with this truth: *I will praise Him for I am fearfully and wonderfully made:*

marvelous are thy works; and that my soul knoweth right well.[19]

• Third, it is important to note how Hannah responded.

This dynamic woman understood that her Creator was her source of worth. She had no significance of her own. Not Eli—nor anyone else— could take away that which she did not possess. Therefore, she did not feel threatened by his error. His opinion was simply not relative to her sense of well being.

Notice what came out of Hannah when pressured by Eli. She respectfully addressed the elderly priest as "my lord." She acknowledged that he, also, was God's handiwork.

Hannah's calm, respectful response was a manifestation of her inner peace. Her godly character was demonstrated by the absence of a contentious spirit. She was at peace with herself as God's creation and was, therefore, able to turn a potentially explosive situation into a simple, peaceful dialog. When her inner peace affected those around her, she became a *peacemaker*.

Note this same exemplary spirit was manifested when Hannah was confronted by Elkanah. Likewise, the stinging darts of Peninnah were repelled,[20] not in a fit of rage or counter accusations, but by a faithful, peaceful spirit. Hannah simply did not answer her.[21]

Hannah clearly acknowledged the Lord as the source of her worth. Her request for a son was a manifestation of that acknowledgement.

We see, then, that the foundation for a peaceful spirit is the acknowledgement of God as our source of personal worth. In the next chapter, we'll build on this foundation. We will learn how acknowledging our true worth enables us to endure persecution.

1. Romans 15:7
2. Proverbs 25:11
3. Romans 14:19
4. II Corinthians 2:11
5. Romans 1:19
6. Ephesians 2:10
7. Galatians 1:15; Psalm 22:10
8. Romans 9:20-21
9. II Timothy 2:25,26; I Peter 5:8,9
10. II Corinthians 10:12
11. Romans 12:12
12. James 2:2-4
13. I Samuel 1:14;15
14. Job 2:3-6; I Peter 5:8
15. James 4:7
16. John 4:24
17. Matthew 4:4,7;10
18. John 8:32
19. Psalm 139:14
20. Ephesians 6:16
21. II Timothy 2:23

Chapter 9

Hannah's Endurance

"Eeeeeeeyuck!"

Parade or no parade, I was *not* going to eat liver and onions.

My father, of course, had a different opinion. And so, in a non-threatening manner, he pointed his fork from across the kitchen table and demanded, "Eat what is set before you!"

I sat there swinging my 4-year-old legs as I stared at the plate.

What made matters worse was seeing Davy Crockett—a.k.a. my older brother, Dave, in his raccoon hat—gulping down his liver and onions like ice cream. He wiped away his milk mustache and pointed his fork in a fatherly fashion. "If you don't eat, you won't be able to go with us to the Race Day Parade!"

Mashed potatoes? Yuck! Asparagus? Yuck! Peas? Then I had an idea. I scooped up three or four peas on my fork.

"Mom!" I said, "Look! I can't eat these peas."

"Why not?" she wondered.

"They won't stay on my fork! They keep rolling off!" With a slight twitch of my wrist, sure enough, they tumbled back to the plate.

My mother was not a preacher, but my act of insolence prompted a short, three-point, one-on-one sermon. Those points included slaving in a hot kitchen, the value of nutrition and something about hungry children in Third World countries. The text, *Foolishness is bound in the heart of a child; but the rod of correction shall drive it far from him,*[1] was most convicting, particularly in an era when corporal punishment was still very much in vogue.

So, I reluctantly ate what was set before me. Within a few moments, I was whisked away to Dad's idling blue '55 Bel Aire and our family drove off to watch the parade.

ଓ THOU PREPAREST A TABLE

Our Heavenly Father also sets a table by placing circumstances before us. He doesn't always prepare situations that *taste* good, but He does promise those that will *be* good.[2]

Occasionally, we cry and whine to the Lord, much as I did to Dad back in 1957. "Heavenly Father," we pray, "why did You allow rejection in my life? I don't like it."

A few times I have even resorted to the peas-falling-off-the-fork tactic. "Lord," I complain, "I just can't handle this. See? It isn't working." Usually He brings to mind some brother or sister in Christ who is cheerfully enduring similar trials.

Sometimes the Lord will set our table with persecution.

Why does our Heavenly Father set our table with perse-cution? Doesn't He know it doesn't taste good?

There is a reason. Persecution not only gives us the privilege of depending on His grace,[3] but it allows our enemies to see Christ through our endurance. Perhaps this is what David had in mind when he wrote in Psalm 23, *Thou preparest a table before me in the presence of mine enemies.*

Consider Hannah's example. God's grace allowed her to endure a table spread with rejection and garnished with disappointment. Rather than wrestle with flesh and blood by trading barbs with her persecutors,[4] Hannah pleaded with the Lord. Her spiritual stamina enabled her to overcome evil with good and prepared her for God's richest blessings. Because of her endurance, those inflicting the pain witnessed God working in her life.

❧ SWITCHBLADE OR SCALPEL?

In Proverbs 26:22, Solomon describes the wounding enemy. *The words of a talebearer,* he wrote, *are as wounds, and they go down into the innermost parts of the belly.*

Then, in Proverbs 27:6, he adds, *Faithful are the wounds of a friend.*

What is the difference between the enemy and the friend? Both cause wounds. Why is the one's wound hurtful while the other is faithful?

The first, I describe as a "wounding thief." His instrument of choice is a switchblade. The second,

I call a "wounding physician." His instrument of choice is a scalpel.

Discerning the difference between a wounding thief and a wounding physician is essential if we are to endure persecution.

The wounding thief haunts the dark alleys of gossip and slander. He preys on unwary victims with no regard for pain. His words slash *down into the innermost parts of the belly.* His intent is to destroy.

The wounding physician works in the light of God's Holy Word. He prays for his patients and is careful to apply soothing balms of comfort and encouragement. His *pleasant words are as an honeycomb, sweet to the soul, and health to the bones.*[5] His desire is to heal.

❧ OVERCOMING EVIL WITH GOOD

Recently, I was robbed at a local bank. Normally, it is the teller who fears being robbed by a customer. This time it was me, the customer, being robbed by the teller. She didn't attempt to steal my money. Rather, she tried to steal my *worth.*

Somehow, in her mind, her caustic behavior, rude manners, and hateful words were draining my sense of personal value and, in doing so, enhancing her own sense of self-esteem. In essence, she was withdrawing from *my personal worth account* and depositing in *her personal worth account*.

My natural response was to take it back!

I deprived her the satisfaction of knowing she was causing emotional discomfort. Instead, I maintained my composure, responded politely, and left her with my best born-again Christian smile. Inside, however, I was wounded to "the innermost parts."

My natural response was to take it back!

I was determined to get even. She had stolen worth from me, now I was going to take it from her; eye for eye, tooth for tooth,[6] and worth for worth.

As I booted my computer, I rehearsed a "Dear Manager" letter in my mind.

The Holy Spirit, however, would have none of it. He reminded me that, only two weeks earlier, I had been in the same bank. A clerk had taken time from her busy schedule to demonstrate their new online banking program. Not only so, but three other bank employees had gathered around to assist in the demonstration. "Isn't it strange," the Holy Spirit seemed to counsel, "that it never occurred to you write a letter *thanking* the manager for their kindness?"

And so I wrote my "Dear Manager" letter—but not as I originally intended. Rather than lambasting the rude teller, I related the pleasant experience of being so well-treated. I also complimented the workers' character, raved about their employee training program and encouraged the manager to keep up the good work.

The next time I visited the bank, I was greeted with more smiles than ever before.

The next time I visited the bank, I was greeted with more smiles than ever before. One teller nudged me, winked and—with a grin—whispered, "We got your letter!"

∞ STEALING WORTH

As mentioned in the previous chapter, God has designed each of us with a healthy desire for a sense of personal worth. We need to know that we are loved, that we have value, and that we have a place in the proverbial scheme of things.

Some folks will try to obtain a sense of value through acquiring money or prestige. Nearly everyone, like the bank teller, attempts to add worth by stealing it from others! They jockey for position on the motorway, fight for the best parking space, then cut in line at the grocery store. By their actions they are saying, "I am hungry for a sense of significance. Therefore, I will steal from others to satisfy my emptiness."

Some find it convenient to steal worth through criticism. I call it "backward bragging." These wounding thieves are seldom so gauche as to steal worth by plainly announcing, "I am smarter than you." Instead, they trumpet the errors of others. In doing so, they are indirectly stating, "I noticed an error that you did not see. Therefore, I am better than you. I am of greater value." Then, through exaggeration, they elevate themselves even higher.

Everywhere, in every walk of life, stealing worth by criticizing others is a natural human pastime. And the church is no exception.

One pastor recalled the story of a listener who was writing feverishly during his sermon. At first, the minister was impressed with the parishioner. He thought she was taking notes of his preaching.

After the service, however, the dear lady approached the minister and presented him with a list of his grammatical errors. When the pastor asked her opinion of the sermon's subject matter, she had none to offer. She hadn't been listening for a message, just for its mistakes. What was her objective? To appear superior to the preacher. Like the bank teller, she attempted to add to her own sense of personal worth by taking it from another.

Stealing worth is ultimately sinful. Why? Because the advancement of self—at the expense of others—is void of God's selfless love. *Giving* worth, by contrast, is a signature of godliness. Jesus noted this distinction when He taught, *By this shall all men know that ye are my disciples, if ye have love one to another.*[7] Paul later reflected this principle when he wrote, *in lowliness of mind let each esteem other better than themselves.*[8] He was effectively saying, "Be a healing physician."

ca GIVING WORTH

Mature Christians understand that they have no importance of their own and, therefore, have nothing that wounding thieves can steal. They have, therefore, no need to jealously guard personal worth. Like Hannah, they are sorrowful when others persecute them with cutting words and selfish actions. Yet they are able to endure that persecution.

Here's why.

An infinite God bestows His worth upon us. There is no need to seek additional value from any other source. Instead, we have an overabundance from which to freely give to others.

Think about the above paragraph!

What are we to do when wounding thieves attempt to steal worth from us? We are to give them more than they are taking!

Therefore, if thine enemy hunger, feed him; if he thirst, give him drink.[9] In doing so, we are demonstrating the unlimited grace of God.

This is the principle taught by Jesus in Matthew 5:39, *but whosoever shall smite thee on thy right cheek, turn to him the other also.*

We endure the persecution of wounding thieves by becoming healing physicians.

ꝏ THE EXTRA MILE

In ancient times, Roman soldiers had the lawful right to force any man, age fourteen or older, to carry their heavy backpacks up to one mile. As a conquered people, the citizens of Israel deplored this law. It was highly offensive because it denigrated their dignity. It stole their worth. When the followers of Jesus willingly carried the packs for one mile, their gracious spirits could not be distinguished from those who grudgingly carried the packs the same distance. Therefore, Jesus instructed his disciples to go one extra mile.[10]

Imagine the surprise of a soldier when he attempted to retrieve his pack after one mile and the Christian just kept on going! Not only was their worth not stolen, the Christians gave additional worth. In doing so their dignity was more than preserved; it was enhanced!

Sometime later I evaluated my experience with the rude bank teller. The Lord had set my table with an unpleasant circumstance. It didn't taste good, but it was for good.

It was good because the squeeze of that situation allowed me to consider what was inside me by asking: Did I resist evil and turn the other cheek?[11] Did I choose to not avenge myself? Did I overcome evil with good?[12]

This is the principle behind Matthew 5:40. If one seeks to take your coat, give it to him—and your cloak also! I challenge you to discover the blessings of freely giving away God's worth.

As we endure what God sets before us, we demonstrate His power within us. Like Hannah, we position ourselves for effective praying.

1. Proverbs 22:15

2. Romans 8:28

3. I Thessalonians 1:6,7

4. Ephesians 6:12

5. Proverbs 16:24

6. Matthew 5:38

7. John 13:35

8. Philippians 2:3

9. Romans 12:20

10. Matthew 5:41

11. Matthew 5:39

12. Romans 12:17,19;21

Chapter 10

Hannah Surrendered

The photograph had been tucked away in a box of cherished family treasures—curios, knick-knacks, keepsakes and the like—hidden on the closet shelf for years. Not until she moved the box aside to make room for her summer shoes did it escape its resting-place.

It fluttered downward like a spinning autumn leaf resting, finally, on the bedroom floor. At first she ignored it. She would retrieve it later. After all, she planned to spend the afternoon cleaning the closet and didn't care to climb down her stepladder. Not for one little picture.

Curiosity, of course, required just one look. Whose picture was it? she wondered. She tilted her head just enough to catch a passing, inquisitive glimpse. She was immediately captured by the gaze of two innocent eyes looking upward from a snapshot of yesteryear. It seemed almost surreal— the little girl stoically grinning from ear to ear.

Stepping from the ladder, she gently lifted the picture, then held it close to absorb every detail of the still, small image. It was a solitary moment from her childhood; a single second snatched from the pinion of time and engraved forever on Kodak's finest.

How could she forget those pigtails? And the tiny hands! Were they really hers? She smiled. Whatever happened to that little girl who was once me?

The closet could wait.

Slowly, she lowered herself to the bedroom floor. Sitting comfortably with her back firmly propped against the bed, she continued to gaze at the photograph. Time's erosion of precious memories seemed to be, at least for the moment, a grievous injustice.

Like a warm cup of tea, she cradled the photo in both hands and searched the shadows of her mind as if to call each cherished memory from its hiding place. One by one they emerged from the misty recesses of time forgotten. She recalled the old house, the neighborhood, and wondered about the friends and neighbors. She remembered her family; the way things were when she was little. There were the dog, the doll, the sidewalk chalk, the sounds of silly songs and the feel of Silly Putty rolled up in her hands. There were senseless rhymes, riddles, bubble baths and Dad's old car. The little girl's smile was reassuring.

Yes, there she was. The shy child she used to be; awkward and naive, yet bold enough to face the challenges of her young life.

She looked into her eyes. "You made it," she caught herself whispering to the picture.

At first she was slightly embarrassed. But then, again, no one was home but her. Who would know? The little girl, of course, retained her pose. She did not reply but, somehow, seemed to hear every word.

She touched the photo with her finger, as if to stroke the little girl's hair. "A few bumps and bruises along the way, but you'll be all right," she advised. "You're gonna cry when you dog dies," she thought a moment, "and your goldfish. But don't worry. It'll be OK."

There was a bandage on the little girl's knee. She remembered the scrape and, my, did it ever hurt. Unconsciously she rubbed her own knee. The scar was still there.

"And don't be afraid when you turn twelve. There will be pimples and bad-hair days. And, uh," she smiled a little broader. "There will be boys. By the way, there's one real heartbreaker I gotta warn you about. This guy's gonna be a major letdown. Be sure to run when you see this tall, dark-haired…"

Then she stopped and giggled. She couldn't believe she was actually giving herself advice, as if it could possibly make a difference.

One last word. "You'll do just fine," she added. "Just keep the faith!"

She reached behind her head and retrieved the Bible she kept on the foot of the bed. Gently, she opened its leafy pages and tucked the photograph inside for safe keeping.

Drawing a deep breath, she stared into nothingness. More memories came; more than she anticipated. The painful relationships, the disappointments in people, the financial struggles. Memories of great expectations were taunted by the stark realities of life; life as it *really* had been.

The smile that graced her countenance surrendered to a thoughtful frown. There *had* been difficulties along the way, more than she cared to remember. A single tear softened the glow of her eye. She pondered the expanse of time that bridged the gap between then and now, and she wondered why God would allow that innocent little girl to endure so many heartaches over so many years.

She continued to thumb through her Bible. Thoughtlessly, at first. Then, purposely. She opened its pages for one last look at the photograph.

And she was in bitterness of soul, and prayed unto the LORD, and wept sore. The words leaped from the page. Another woman from another generation and other place, feeling the same hurt; knowing the same heartache. She smiled—again—through her tears. Hannah must have been cleaning her closet, she thought.

She continued to read.

> *O LORD of hosts*
> *if thou wilt indeed*
> *look on the affliction of thine handmaid,*
> *and remember me,*
> *and not forget thine handmaid,*
> *but wilt give unto thine handmaid a man child,*
> *then I will give him unto the LORD*
> *all the days of his life.*

Hannah gave it to the Lord, she considered. Not just her son, but her sorrow—and her hope of joy. She simply gave it all to the Lord!

The thought was refreshing.

And so, with head bowed, she whispered a prayer of surrender—her own prayer of Hannah.

"Heavenly Father, grant me the courage of Hannah. I give you now my past with all its hurts and all its joys. And I give you my future. My plans, my dreams; my desires. If you choose to return them to me, I will dedicate them for you *all the days of my life.* In Jesus name. Amen."[1]

✂ THE SURRENDERED LIFE

She discovered the most basic principle of effective Christianity: the willingness to sacrifice everything.[2] It is to relinquish those things that God has permitted—the good and the bad; our victories and defeats, our strengths and weaknesses—and return them to Him. *All* of them. Every experience, possession and moment of time becomes our "Samuel". We are no longer owners, but stewards. Our passions cease to be centered on self. They focus, instead, on Him.

Effective praying is the result of effective Christianity. It begins when we give our past, our present and our future to the Lord. It cares nothing for one's reputation, but everything for God's kingdom. It seeks His righteousness first and foremost.

We are no longer owners, but stewards.

Because there is nothing in effective praying that advances one's personal will, it excludes selfish ambition to embrace heavenly direction. It never asks, "My will be done in heaven as it is on earth." Such selfish praying presumes that

Almighty God is nothing more than a talisman or a genie in bottle. Such is the essence of praying amiss.[3]

Rather, effective praying seeks the will of God *as it is in heaven*[4]—not in the formulated arrangement of words, but in a dedicated submission of the heart. Then, submitted to that will, it cries aloud that it would be accomplished on earth.[5]

ભ THE SUPREME OBJECTIVE

A surrendered spirit, then, is the essence of powerful praying. Why? Because it focuses not on personal gain, but determines to do nothing more—and nothing less—than bring glory to God. Even when concerned with cares of life, it never strays from that supreme objective.

Consider, for example, the prayer of Moses.

When pleading with an angry God to pardon his rebellious congregation, Moses made this appeal from their wilderness wandering: *Wherefore should the Egyptians speak, and say, For mischief did he bring them out, to slay them in the mountains, and to consume them from the face of the earth?*[6]

His prayer was answered. God was glorified by revealing His great mercy as *the LORD repented of the evil which he thought to do unto his people.*[7]

Elijah prayed these simple words, *LORD God of Abraham, Isaac, and of Israel, let it be known this day that thou art God in Israel, and that I am thy servant*[8]—and fire fell from heaven! This great prophet of old sought the glory of God.

The prayer of Nehemiah, likewise, sought the glory of the Lord. He understood that God's ear is attentive to those who fear his name, not those who seek selfish ambition. He prayed, *O LORD, I beseech thee, let now thine ear be attentive to the prayer of thy servant, and to the prayer of thy servants, who desire to fear thy name: and prosper, I pray thee, thy servant this day, and grant him mercy in the sight of this man.*[9]

Yet all were committed—first and foremost—to appeal to God's glory.

Dynamic Christianity sees every adversity as a pretext for prayer. Each heartache is a blessed privilege to seek the Lord's intervention and every sorrow an occasion for God to be glorified.

Moses recognized that occasion as he interceded for his people. Elijah put his testimony on the line—to the glory of God.[9]   Nehemiah forthrightly asked for prosperity—that God would be glorified. Just prior to raising Lazarus from the dead, Jesus, Himself, declared, *This sickness is...for the glory of God.*[10]

Empowered with this confidence,[11] one can boldly take heaven by force,[12] stand in the presence of an omnipotent God and be showered with the blessings of answered prayer.

Such was the prayer of Hannah.

Eight spiritual dynamics can be seen in the foundation of Hannah's effective praying. The first four were steps of character development; the latter four demonstrated that character.

∞ EIGHT SPIRITUAL DYNAMICS

• First Dynamic—Hannah was humbled.

With a spirit of humility, she abandoned even the shadow of selfish desire. In so doing, she sacrificed that which was most precious in her sight to the glory of God.

• Second Dynamic—Hannah was broken.

Her humility allowed her— like soft clay in the Potter's hand—to be fashioned through brokenness for the purpose of usefulness.[13] Every disappointment, tear and heartache were strokes of the Master's hand forming a vessel to His glory.

• Third Dynamic—Hannah was strengthened.

God *always* instills His vessels with the strength to endure those tasks for which they were created.[14] Meekness is the mere recognition of that strength. It submits one's own abilities and—instead—depends wholly on the strength of the Potter. It rests securely on the Father's shoulders and thrills at the blessing of a godly perspective.

• Fourth Dynamic—Hannah had godly desire.

Her prayer also reveals a yearning to do the will of the Lord. It evidentially defines a woman who was after the heart of God. Hannah would settle for nothing less than His power in her life. Having tasted the blessed life she would not be distracted by meager human appetites.

• Fifth dynamic—Hannah was merciful.

She surrendered her reputation to become God's servant—mighty in spirit; mighty in prayer.

• Sixth dynamic—Hannah was at peace.

Her worth was limited to nothing less than the infinite grace of God. It not only gave her a peace that could not be stolen by her adversaries, but afforded her the privilege of imparting it to others. In doing so, Hannah became a peacemaker.

• Seventh dynamic—Hannah was pure.

Peninnah was opaque. God could not be seen through her. Elkanah and Eli were transluscent The glory of God was evident, but not clearly seen. Hannah was transparent. Even today, Her purity continues to allow God to be abundantly evident through her testimony.

• Eighth dynamic—Hannah endured.

She was grateful for the table spread before her. She ran, but never grew weary. She walked, without fainting. And, ultimately, she rejoiced![15]

Surrender allows us to embrace the privilege of spiritual growth. Humility, brokenness, meekness and godly desire—once perceived as foolishness—are welcomed as the foundation of godly character. It then grants us the privilege of expressing that character through mercy, peace, purity and endurance.

As these eight dynamics are integrated into our lives, God will be glorified and we will be blessed—guaranteed![16]

1. Kenny Paul Clarkson, *Back Home in Round Hill*, Just Folks Publishing Company, Columbus, Indiana, 2002
2. Philippians 3:7
3. James 4:3
4. Matthew 6:10
5. Luke 11:2; Matthew 16:19
6. Exodus 32:12
7. Exodus 32:14
8. 1 Kings 18:36
9. Nehemiah 1:11
10. John 11:4
11. 1 John 5:14
12. Matthew 11:12
13. Mark 14:3, for example
14. 2 Timothy 2:21
15. 1 Samuel 2:1-10
16. Matthew 5:2-12

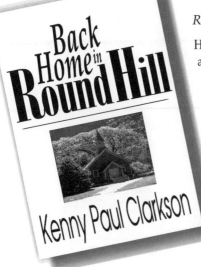